CONFESS

SUSAN TEPPER

Červená Barva Press
Somerville, Massachusetts

Červená Barva Press
P.O. Box 440357
W. Somerville, MA 02144-3222

www.cervenabarvapress.com

Bookstore: www.thelostbookshelf.com

Cover Image: Violetta © Marie Lynam Fitzpatrick, Oil on Canvas, 2018

Author photo: A. j. Savastinuk

Cover design: William J. Kelle

ISBN: 978-1-950063-38-3

BOOKS BY SUSAN TEPPER

ACKNOWLEDGMENTS

Grateful acknowledgment is made to the following editors for publishing these poems in their fine journals both print and online.

Broken, *Cervena Barva Press*
Desirous, *The Linnet's Wings*
Egg, *Revival Poetry Journal*
Confess, *The Stony Thursday Book*
Each Sky, *TheFirstCut A Literary Journal*
Tangled, *Poetry Salzburg Review*
Deep Snow, *Boyne Berries*
Dark Country, *Grasslimb*
Course, *Cervena Barva Press*
Part & Parcel, *Crannog*
Some Rooms, *River Poets Journal*
Away the Winter, *Ropes*
Beggar's Soup, *The Galway Review*
Solitary, *Poesia*
Hearts, *Lyrical Somerville in The Somerville Times*
Channel, *The Rye Whiskey Review*
Fractured, *READ THIS chapbook, London Poetry Festival*
Where, *Nixes Mate Review*

My utmost thanks and appreciation to Marie Lynam Fitzpatrick for her exquisite Violetta painting which graces the cover of this collection.

TABLE OF CONTENTS

Dedicated to my husband, Miles, with everlasting love

CONFESS

Broken

I come to you broken
have been trying to say
all that is not the way
it shows on the surface—
a lake I carry on my back
one of stillness
lifted from some old photo
from a book, when the cover
matched the insides when girls
pretended to be women
and vice-versa:
they wore hats on Easter
and carried lit candles up flocks
of stairs like birds

Desirous

Your heart envies its factions
choruses of deliverance
that keep failing

despite a clutching effort

to hold intact what is left
the slightest drop of good will
You are your own prisoner

desirous of this place

your cries for help go rigid
in a black-tinged scarlet night

tongue of nights that pass over
any light that could be cast
by a new moon

Egg

The beams swollen with water
fear the ceiling's collapse from
the weight of her belly

So far the child is curled up
safe before the awakening

The cottage still,
though here and there
a beam creaks like it's tired

strapped centuries in one place

Sweet baby – finally set free,
the egg tumbles into the straw

Confess
you're hungry, scrape the plate
wait for darkness to settle its glove
on your mouth, a sigh, a whisper

They come and go, you know this
before it started, the clouds
opening and a small sun

round as a dime
hurts when you lick its edges—
confess

Call to the owl you hear every night
in the tree's blue shadow

Each Sky

Don't break down my door
the wood is soft, will turn to
crumbs you'll want to eat

that's how much sweetness

But— wait!
what's the hurry

Another storm moving across
each sky is a belt
growing tighter

and you try
breathing the stories in—

Tangled

Scrape my face— find
vines and what I want

leave tangled—
there were countries

cut in sections
viable yet invisible
but for leanings— a shoulder

against a train window

raindrops blinding trees
beyond the reach of
what was cold

You clutched a coat,
promised again to be sorry.

Deep Snow

You grip the lamp, alone
The hall and silence—

It is night, afraid
For you, while it has
Fought your every step

Each movement as if
Through deep snow

Your knees wet and frozen
Buckle as the water
Starts to puddle and melt
The long winter.

Dark Country

Two things considered:
both cabbages need slicing

cut in half like heads left
after a revolution

the kitchen is a dark country

softened borders, what
remains lurk in corners—

you asked to read my palm
while I was busy salting fish

a fog horn blared, mist
blinding the windows.

Course

— for Simon Perchik

Shared course: the rivers and the streams
our words come out of their harsh winter—
frost melting edges smoothing
spring's first rush: the birds, shoots;
bristle grass softening to brighter green
— we have learned to take our name
pushed shoreline to shoreline
the wave's force till it crumbles
shells and the hour
the heart meets itself, blankly
hears its name in the crumpled page
its spool running out in the dark.

Part & Parcel

Close the shutters
Allow darkness to rip
Your eyes in tide pools.

Two suitcases, side by side
Have yet to be unpacked.

Excuses, elaborations
Does this mean we won't stay long?

You're flattened by so many roads
I am stung and run over.

Two suitcases: it's been written
Part & Parcel by your own hand.

Some Rooms
                    —for my mother

you could pat down
chairs all smooth
and dusted horse-hair—

mute now, forgot
to say goodbye
give you a smile, remark
that you're pretty

The tall arc lamp
burned a ridge at night
iron-scorched the arms
of the couch

your arms each birthday
take time to
circle the lake

birds dip to plunder

Away the Winter

As with the maple your leaves
come off in silent streams

Litter the bed and on the floor
crunching where you
meant to keep

away the winter

hiding behind curtains
crouched in the rafters

Have you heard the windows
gasp— cold and so dark
surely they have died too.

Beggar's Soup

The old bird is cut up
to put in the beggar's soup.
Deliver my name in vain.
Blood and a bit of celery
add flavor to the stock.
I recall flying low
over a bright beach
following the shoreline.
It was a cascade of
party boats dotted with
a few trawlers.
Here and there house boats
with chairs outside.

Solitary

You will forget a darkened room
grey as a four o'clock winter's day

outside streets were baking
ninety and hands on ankles
refusing to listen
you ticked a broken clock

the slippery cream
hiding a tree or a river
gone solitary in its confinement.

August, Paris

Across the café table a man is drowning,
my beloved, here I met, so help me.
Water had risen to the tops of his eyes,
not a miracle or sacrifice
nor even simple tears
but the springs of who he was,
before he formed,
who he would become,
the eventual suffering into later life.
It ripped me. In such a way
as could not be explained or rationalized.
I saw the light would drown him.
Grey over the coming winter into spring.
I sat perfectly still, aging in a hotel mirror.

Hearts

Determined to stop all feeling
we drive our hearts
deep into winter

as if they are the hearts
of vampires

And, we, the mighty
possessed of hammer & stake
have the right to banish
this crude interloper

this heart
done-up in scarlet, no less—

A fusion of veins and vessel of
dreams sweet and bitter
this heart

destined to follow its
natural course

dragging bewildered body
behind in its wake,
or simply sitting still
as a statue in the park.

Dare we sentence it
to wither
alone
in dank chambers

Channel

Bury me in a giant keg, I'm lonely—
the squeeze of amniotic
fluid waves made seminal
a twin who didn't escape
the narrow channel—
Question on whisky lips
always pondering
the why— in the end
a reason for
hugging dark bars
in daylight with other dead people.

Fractured
you spend the night
addressing the wind
in foreign tongues

make bloody the sheets
and pillowcases to shreds
your teeth are blind

the bedroom in tatters

despite floating seafoam walls
the deep-pink blooms of
ancient origins drifting across
— the way stars outside your window

Where

Your arms hold secrets
the papers destroyed
white envelopes
folded
as you would
love letters or a list —
Could be simple
milk, eggs, tea
Or could be the part
where you stop to think:
where have I been

About the Author

Susan Tepper grew up amidst the dairy farms and wild strawberry fields of Long Island, when it was still a mystical finger in the water. A multitude of careers that include actress, singer, flight attendant, airline marketing manager, Cable TV producer, overseas tour guide, interior decorator, rescue worker and more have informed her poetry and fiction. An award-winning author, Tepper lives with her husband in the New York area. For more information please visit www.susantepper.com

A Special Thanks

"For some twenty years now, I have been truly blessed to call poet Simon Perchik my close friend. We met by chance, or perhaps not. Simon brought me and Gloria Mindock together. Another blessing. Si's great sense of humor, his brilliance as a poet, and his deep compassion for the world help fuel me as person and writer."
— Susan Tepper, January 25, 2020